FREQUENTLY ASKED QUESTIONS ABOUT

Butterflies

Common buckeye

ROSE HOUK

Western National Parks Association

Tucson, Arizona

Why are they called "butterflies"?

The word "butterflies" may come from the Old English *buterfleoge* or from a species named the "butter-colored fly" or a less attractive suggestion, (for such beautiful creatures) from the Dutch term *boterschijte*, referring to the color of their excrement.

How many species of butterflies are there?

Entomologists know of about 18,000 butterfly species worldwide, living on all continents except Antarctica. About 600 species flutter about the western United States, west of the 100th Meridian. Texas ranks first, Arizona second, and New Mexico third in total number of species in the United States. In the western United States, the variety of habitats and life zones means a great richness in the kinds of butterflies found there.

How are butterflies classified?

Butterflies are insects in the order Lepidoptera, or "scale wing." The overlapping scales that cover their wings and bodies are the defining characteristic. Butterflies account for an estimated 5 percent of the Lepidoptera, while moths make up the rest. There are six butterfly families in the western United States: swallowtails, whites and sulfurs, gossamer wings, metalmarks, brushfoots, and skippers. They are known by a rich lexicon of common names: monarchs and queens, viceroys and admirals, question marks and commas, satyrs and nymphs.

The West has many different life zones and butterfly habitats.

When did butterflies originate?

Fewer than 50 butterfly fossils are known, because these insects are so fragile and unlikely to be preserved. By 66 million years ago, modern butterfly families likely had developed, coinciding with the development of flowering plants. Paleontologists have uncovered the majority of butterfly fossils in rock less than 50 million years old. Florissant Fossil Beds National Monument in Colorado is famed for fossil butterflies. The finely preserved specimens, which include rare caterpillar fossils, are encased in 34-million-year-old rock. At Florissant the rock, or minerals in it, have been dated rather than the fossils themselves.

Antennae can be a good way to tell moths from butterflies. The tiger moth (left) has feather-like antennae, while the Atlantis fritillary butterfly (right) has round-tipped antennae.

What is the difference between a butterfly and a moth?

One of the best ways to distinguish butterflies from moths is by their antennae. Butterfly antennae have club-shaped or rounded tips, while moth antennae are featherlike. Generally butterflies fly in daytime, moths fly at night. Butterflies are usually larger and more brightly colored than moths. Butterfly caterpillars eat voraciously for two weeks or so, while moth caterpillars feed for weeks or months. Moth chrysalises are wrapped in silk cocoons, but butterfly chrysalises are hardened protective cases without silk. These distinctions blur, however. For example, the skippers are butterflies that exhibit some moth like characteristics, and some subtropical butterflies are active at night.

A bramble hairstreak butterfly

What is the range of sizes among butterflies?

The American western pygmy blue may be the smallest butterfly, with a wingspan of about 1/2 inch. The largest butterfly in the world is the Queen Alexandra's birdwing of New Guinea. The female's wings stretch to nearly a foot wide.

The western pygmy blue may be the smallest butterfly.

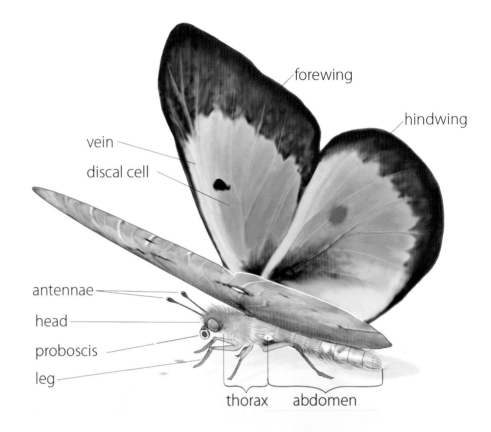

What are the major parts of butterfly anatomy?

Butterflies are insects with three body sections—head, thorax, and abdomen. They have six true legs and external skeletons. All butterflies have two pairs of wings, called forewings and hindwings. The hollow veins in the wings serve as structural support, much like struts on an airplane. Butterflies have large compound eyes, two antennae, and a retractable mouthpart called a proboscis that is uncoiled and used like a straw to take up liquids.

COLORS ALLOW BUTTERFLIES TO *distinguish* THEIR OWN KIND FROM OTHER SPECIES.

What makes butterflies so colorful?

Butterflies' colors arise from the scales, both as actual pigments and from a structural, prismatic effect. The colors range from brown, green, and orange to velvety-thick blacks and blues and tissue-thin copper, yellow, white, and silvery blue. Some have iridescent streaks and metallic markings. Others are checkered, spotted, dotted, and intricately veined. With such exquisite colors and markings, it is no wonder that butterflies have been likened to flowers with wings.

Knowledge of coloring and markings can help in butterfly identification. The gulf fritillary has three white dots encircled by black on the leading edge of the upper wings.

What is the purpose for the colors and markings?

Colors allow butterflies to distinguish their own kind from other species. Colors serve as deception, camouflage, or mimicry, while notable markings such as "eyespots" deter predators. Colors and markings can sometimes differentiate males from females of a particular species. In almost all butterflies, patterns and colors on the upper wings are strikingly unlike those on the underwings. When a butterfly perches with wings folded together, the often cryptically colored lower surfaces aid greatly in camouflage. The dark colors of many western butterflies help them warm up under cool conditions.

Where do butterflies live?

Butterflies live in almost every environment—coastal areas, hot deserts, grasslands and prairie, shrublands, woodlands, forests, and even up into high alpine tundra. They can be found in cities and towns, fields and gardens, along roadsides, and in parks and wilderness. Some can live in a variety of habitats, while others have highly specific requirements for temperature, host plants, and nectar sources.

The common buckeye has eyespots that deter predators.

insect's life.

What is the life cycle of a butterfly?

What we think of as a butterfly is just the adult stage of the insect's life. In fact, the adult is totally unlike the organism that hatched from the egg. The complex process called complete metamorphosis occurs in four stages: egg (ovum), caterpillar (larva), chrysalis (pupa), and adult butterfly (imago). The entire cycle for most butterflies takes about a month. Some species go through the cycle once a year, others several times annually. For those in cold climates, at high elevations, or in arid places, the cycle can take two years or more.

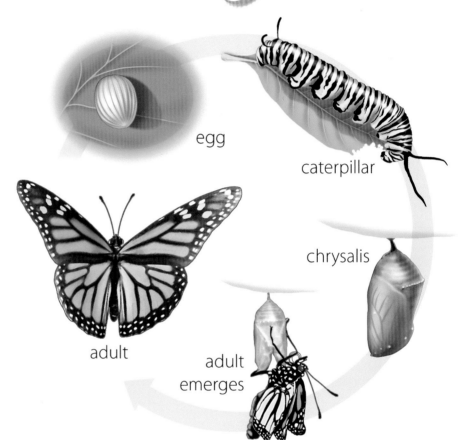

egg

caterpillar

chrysalis

adult

adult emerges

Mourning cloaks can live 10 to 11 months.

How long do butterflies live?

Life span depends on the species. In summer some may live as briefly as a day or a week or two, long enough to breed and for the female to lay all her eggs. Adult fritillaries, checkerspots, and others in the brushfoot family last for months. Mourning cloaks win the award as possibly the longest-lived butterfly. They can live for 10 to 11 months. Adult mourning cloaks rest in summer, feed in the fall, spend the winter under tree bark, and mate the following spring.

1. A female lays her eggs, singly or in clusters, on host plants. She glues them tightly to the surface with substances from her body. Eggs vary remarkably in size and shape, from a small dot to a large spindle. They're covered with strong but porous membranes.

2. The caterpillar, or larva, eats through the egg and crawls out onto a leaf of the plant. Some consume part of the eggshell before beginning to chew on the leaves. Caterpillars have been termed "eating machines," because they gobble green food nearly nonstop for two weeks or so. They shed, or molt, their exoskeletons four to five times during this stage to allow for growth.

3. When the caterpillar stops eating, it prepares to pupate. The caterpillar becomes lethargic, changes colors, and finally stops moving.

4. It spins silk from a specialized gland called a spinneret, guy wires itself to part of a plant, and the pupa forms. (Some larvae drop to the ground and enter the pupa stage there.) The pupa is also called the chrysalis, because shimmering gold or metallic spots adorn the casing on species such as monarchs. ("*Chrysalis*" comes from the Greek word for "gold.") Other pupae are less showy, looking much like a leaf on the plant they hang from.

5. During this resting stage, the caterpillar's tissues liquefy, dissolve, and reorganize into the adult chrysalis.

6. When fully developed, the adult emerges as a butterfly. It takes in air and swells, the chrysalis splits open, and the butterfly pumps fluid into its wings. The butterfly must fully extend its wings within the first hour, or they will harden in the folded position and the butterfly will be unable to fly. That day or the next, females and males take flight in search of mates; they have a very brief time in which to breed.

Orange sulfurs and cloudless sulfurs puddling.

What are some interesting butterfly behaviors?

Butterflies bask in the sun to warm their muscles and dry their wings so that they can fly. They join in "puddle parties" at wet, muddy spots to get fluids, salts, and minerals. These congregations are almost all males. The males also patrol stream edges and other places, on the lookout for females emerging from the chrysalis.

Butterflies also have a habit of "hilltopping," seeking high places where males and females can find each other more easily; similarly, males perch in sunny places at the top of a tree or other high point, defending it against other males and waiting for a female to come by. Male great purple hairstreaks, for example, are known to commandeer palo verde trees for several weeks, the same butterfly returning to the same tree through time.

How do butterflies fly?

As butterflies take off and climb into the air, they use a technique called "clap and peel." The forewings clap together on the upstroke, and the hindwings peel away on the downstroke, giving them lift. Unlike an airplane's fixed wings, butterfly wings are highly flexible and maneuverable, constantly tilting, gliding, and flapping. Ten to 20 wingbeats a second is a rough average, but bigger butterflies may beat their wings more slowly.

Flight allows butterflies to escape predators, find food, avoid bad weather, and colonize new areas. Each butterfly family exhibits characteristic flight patterns, dictated by overall weight, wing size and shape, and the environment. The larger swallowtails possess a powerful stroke; some metalmarks stay still long enough for a person to closely approach; hairstreaks and blues fly fast and frenetically, never seeming to stop in one place for long.

How high, how fast, and how far can they fly?

Migrating or moving with storm fronts, butterflies can reach several thousand feet in altitude, but most average about 2 or 3 feet above the ground. Most butterflies can travel 5 to 12 miles an hour, but in a sprint their top speed could be 50 miles an hour. In terms of distance, a migrating monarch might go 80 miles in a day, but that would be a long distance for any butterfly.

A gray hairstreak takes a rare pause.

Under what conditions can they fly?

As with all insects, butterflies must warm up to the surrounding temperature before they become active. The sun warms their flight muscles and the scales covering their wings. Some orient themselves toward the sun to help the process, and like humans they also shiver to warm up. Ambient temperature needs to be about 55 to 60 degrees before they take flight. Once airborne, butterflies can move to other spots and bask in the sun to raise their body temperatures to the optimum 82 to 100 degrees.

Flight

ALLOWS BUTTERFLIES TO ESCAPE PREDATORS, FIND FOOD, AND AVOID BAD WEATHER.

How do butterflies sense their environment?

Chemical receptors and nerve cells on butterflies' antennae, proboscises, bodies, and even their feet are used to taste and smell. Their sense of touch comes through tiny sensory hairs, called setae, covering their bodies. They have two large compound eyes with thousands of lenses in each. Butterflies are highly sensitive to light and see a wide spectrum of color, from red to near ultraviolet. This helps them detect intricate markings on flowers that lead to pools of nectar, and aids in locating the opposite sex.

Giant swallowtails in courtship ritual

How do butterflies mate?

Each species produces a distinctive pheromone, a chemical that communicates readiness to breed and is detectable from a distance. In the branded skipper and other species, pheromones reside within specialized scales. To assure that the pheromones are communicated, the male does a courtship "dance," flying around and in front of the female, hovering, fluttering, and touching her wings. Some males flourish fringed edges on their wings to dispense the intoxicant. If the female is receptive, the male grasps her abdomen with a clasper. Connected abdomen-to-abdomen, they mate. If disturbed, the two will take flight with one carrying the other still attached.

Cabbage whites mating.

BUTTERFLIES MIMIC EACH OTHER TO AVOID *predators.*

A spider feasts on a skipper.

What is a host plant?

A host plant is the food plant for the larvae, the plant where an adult female lays her eggs, and sometimes the location of the chrysalis. Female butterflies find the requisite host plants by sight and by "tasting" with their feet. The relationship between host plant and caterpillar is highly specific. Some will feed only on one species or one family of plants. Monarch and queen larvae, for instance, require milkweeds. The great blue hairstreak wants mistletoe; certain metalmarks go exclusively to buckwheats, the empress leila to hackberry, and pipevine swallowtails only to pipevines. Other butterflies are more cosmopolitan, selecting ash and citrus, mustards, legumes, or composites. For some species, we haven't yet discovered the host plant.

What are their major predators?

Birds, lizards, frogs, spiders, mammals, and other insects such as wasps and dragonflies commonly prey on butterflies and caterpillars.

How do butterflies help pollinate plants?

When a butterfly lands on a flower, it inserts its proboscis to reach the sweet nectar within the flower. As it does so, pollen from the flower anthers inadvertently sticks to the insect. Visiting other flowers of the same kind, the butterfly carries that pollen there and deposits it.

A monarch butterfly lands on fall garden mums.

What do butterflies eat?

Most adult butterflies dine on flower nectar from many different kinds of flowers. And though nectar (and plant sap) accounts for a good deal of their nutrition, they also choose rotting fruit, carrion, and excrement to obtain salts and other minerals.

The red-spotted purple (left) and the black swallowtail (right) mimic the pipevine swallowtail (center), which is bad-tasting to birds.

How do butterflies avoid predators or defend themselves?

Flight is an obvious defense against those that would eat them. But sitting still is also effective through use of coloration. A butterfly relies on color in two basic ways: subtle camouflage against tree bark and plant foliage, or gaudy colors that shout "I taste bad" or "I'm not the one you want." False eyespots on wings (buckeyes), tails on the wings (swallowtails), and other such foils

will deceive predators. Hairstreaks rub their hindwings together in a motion that distracts predators away from the head and body.

Mimicry is the most sophisticated deceit. Viceroys, in black and orange, strongly resemble the poisonous monarch, so predators stay away from them. Black swallowtails and red-spotted purples mimic the pipevine swallowtail, bad-tasting to birds.

The viceroy (top) closely resembles the poisonous monarch (bottom).

Caterpillars have methods too. Swallowtail larvae flick out a foul-smelling odor from a gland behind their heads to repulse predators, and giant swallowtail caterpillars are cleverly camouflaged as bird droppings. The monarch larva takes up toxins from its milkweed host plant. Those poisons sicken vertebrate predators that eat the caterpillar (but invertebrate predators such as wasps and spiders are immune). Other caterpillars possess sharp, bristly hairs or blend perfectly with their host plant.

Do butterflies have relationships with other insects?

Yes. Most interesting is the beneficial association between certain butterfly larvae and ants. In some blues, for example, the larvae secrete a sugary solution called "honeydew" that attracts at least a dozen species of ants. The ants tend the larvae and protect them from predators; for their efforts, they receive nutrients from the honeydew. Butterfly larvae also benefit by being able to go into ant nests to pupate. But when they change to adults, they must escape or the ants kill them.

Western pygmy blue larvae and ant

A monarch butterfly enduring rain

How does weather affect butterfly activity and numbers?

Butterflies prefer warm, sunny, dry weather. They rarely move about on cloudy, rainy, or cold days. Seasonal temperatures and length of daylight (photoperiod) also affect their movements. Late freezes can stop emerging adults in their tracks. Long droughts can greatly reduce sources of nectar plants and thus their sources of food. The wind can carry numbers of butterflies to a locale, and when it blows hard the delicate butterflies must seek shelter.

What myths and stories surround butterflies?

Butterflies are important symbols to southwestern Pueblo peoples. They are part of complex imagery, appearing as painted designs on pottery and kiva walls and in the words of songs. To the Hopi, butterflies are an integral part of *Siitàlpuva*, the land brightened with flowers. With summer rains, flowers bloom and draw butterflies and birds. Butterflies are messengers of the germination spirit, and are associated with abundance and fertility. Also, young Hopi women wear their hair coiled in butterfly-shaped whorls. The Aztecs believed the butterfly was the manifestation of a god. Their name for it was Xochiqetzalpapalotl, "flower-plumed-serpent-butterfly."

In ancient Greece and Rome, butterflies symbolized the soul or dying. The Greek word for them is *psyche*— "soul" or "breath"—also the name of a goddess. Roman legend spoke of Psyche, who fought with her lover, Cupid. After he left, she searched desperately for him. Jupiter took mercy on her and made her immortal. In Latin, *papilio* relates to souls that return in the form of butterflies. Butterflies decorated the tombs of Egyptian pharaohs, and people of the Middle Ages believed butterflies were fairies that stole food.

BUTTERFLIES ARE IMPORTANT *symbols* TO SOUTHWESTERN PUEBLO PEOPLES.

What do butterflies do when it gets too cold or too hot?

A few species can survive extreme cold by hibernating or going dormant. If it gets too hot, some enter a dormancy period called "estivation." During these times of pause, they slow or interrupt their development, growth, or metamorphosis.

Some species such as monarchs and painted ladies migrate. Monarch migrations—the longest of any butterfly—have garnered a great deal of attention. Two groups migrate. In the fall monarchs east of the Rocky Mountains fly some 2,500 miles from north to south, funneling through Texas into Mexico, where millions of

Monarchs have the longest migration of any butterfly.

them gather in mountains west of Mexico City. Those west of the Rockies head to the coast of California for the winter, or a few travel to warmer areas in Arizona and New Mexico. It is now known that some of those also go south to the overwintering area in Mexico.

In spring the monarchs head north again. But those that make the return flight are first- and second-generation individuals. The big mystery surrounding this spectacular movement is how these offspring find their way back to the same overwintering sites every year. They may use topographical landmarks and the angle of the sun, or they may have internal compasses. Researchers have also found that monarchs possess a unique "biological clock," allowing them to keep a correct and fixed bearing in flight, using the sun as a compass.

A study in the Southwest aims to find out if monarchs reside in the region all year, or if they migrate as well. In the fall, when most monarchs are seen in greater numbers, workers net them, apply a small blue numbered tag to the hindwing, and assemble information through a network of observers.

N

ROCKY MOUNTAINS

SUMMER

SUMMER

WINTER

SPRING

WINTER

Mexico City

WINTER

MONARCH MIGRATIONS

→ Fall

← Spring/Summer

? Unconfirmed route

Research courtesy of Monarch Watch

Irruptions

OCCUR WHEN CONDITIONS
ARE CONDUCIVE TO SURVIVAL.

Why do some butterflies suddenly increase in numbers?
Large increases in populations—called irruptions—may be due to favorable weather or fewer predators and parasites. They can occur from year to year or seasonally when conditions are conducive to survival. When numbers become excessive, however, butterflies can outstrip available food sources and must mass-disperse.

The bordered patch and the American snout are two species known for irruptions. One female can lay hundreds of eggs, then weeks later the butterfly population explodes.

How do butterflies serve as environmental barometers?
Because of their close association with plants, butterflies respond quickly if they lose host plants or overall habitat. And with the importance of ambient temperature to their flight and behavior, they are susceptible to climate change. Whether they will be able to adapt quickly enough is a huge question. Some, such as Edith's checkerspot, have already shown significant upward and northward movements in their ranges, but not every species can be as responsive or flexible.

The American snout is a species known for irruptions.

What are the biggest threats to butterflies, and what species are rare or endangered?

Some butterfly species are naturally rare and have very small ranges, leaving them vulnerable. Others have been victims of habitat loss, overgrazing, development, and recreational damage. Deforestation has already occurred on one of 12 mountaintops where monarchs overwinter in Mexico. Herbicides can wipe out host plants, and some genetically altered crops contain deadly toxins. Overcollecting (and smuggling) is an issue.

Among western species of concern is the endangered El Segundo blue. It lives in sandy places in southern California, with one key population protected just beyond the runways of Los Angeles International Airport. Through its life cycle, this blue is tied to the flowers of the seacliff buckwheat.

The small, pale Mojave dotted blue needs wild buckwheats as host plants. The dry, sandy washes of the Mojave Desert where it lives are being invaded by exotic, fireprone cheatgrass, leaving this butterfly without its native food source.

Dakota and ottoe skippers, species of the Great Plains and prairies, have seen their native habitat greatly diminished by agricultural

Some butterfly species are naturally rare and have very small ranges, leaving them vulnerable.

development, pesticides, and invading species. The larvae need little bluestem or other grasses, and the adults want coneflowers and other prairie flowers for nectar.

Citizens, governments, and conservation groups have helped with protection and recovery efforts. Across the country, individuals and communities are planting native gardens with host and nectar plants to attract butterflies. Nonprofit groups are working to restore populations of rare and threatened butterflies in North America. We still have much

The Huachuca giant skipper lives only in woodlands of pine, oak, and juniper in the Huachuca and Chiricahua mountains in southern Arizona and in the "sky island" mountains of northern Mexico. It depends on Parry's agave as a host plant. Livestock grazing and wildfire threaten its specialized habitat.

more to learn about the particular needs of many butterfly species. And, new species are still being discovered.

When is the best time to see butterflies?

Butterflying is always best on a bright sunny day. Elevation and season also figure in. Some butterflies are out only in the summer months, others in lower-elevation deserts fly early in the year, some even year-round. In the Southwest the phenomenon of summer monsoon rains from July through September brings large numbers of butterflies. In drainages and on mountains of the borderlands, Mexican species often come north as the rains bring a flush of flowers.

Western tailed blue

Is it harmful to release butterflies for ceremonies?

Yes. Releasing live butterflies at weddings and other events is not recommended because if they're not native to the area, commercially raised butterflies may mix inappropriately with local species and spread diseases. Also many do not survive transport, and if they do they may not find the necessary plant foods in the new habitat either.

Where can I go to see butterflies and get more information about them?

Just about any flower-filled place, even your own backyard or neighborhood park will have butterflies. You can also venture farther afield to national parks, forests, wildlife refuges, and preserves. Many arboretums and public gardens throughout the West feature butterfly houses and exhibits. In addition, organizations such as the North American Butterfly Association and local chapters; the Lepidopterists' Society; and other regional groups meet and offer field trips devoted to butterflies.

Why watch butterflies?

Author and naturalist Robert Michael Pyle has answered this question well. He writes, "In a jaded world, butterfly watching furnishes a simple and refreshing pathway to fascination." Beyond appreciation of their sheer beauty, butterflies can lead us to a greater appreciation and care for our native landscapes, and help us establish or reestablish a link to the natural world.

What is the best way to view butterflies?

Simply going out and watching butterflies is a first step. As with birding, close-focus binoculars and a good field guide help in observing and identifying them. And photographing them is the ideal way to "net" a sighting.

A giant swallowtail butterfly flies in for nectar.

Learn More

Butterfly Conservation Initiative
www.butterflyrecovery.org

**Butterflies and Moths
of North America**
www.butterfliesandmoths.org

Monarch Watch
www.monarchwatch.org

Xerces Society
www.xerces.org

Milbert's tortoiseshell

Further Reading

Bailowitz, Richard and Hank Brodkin. *Finding Butterflies in Arizona.* Johnson Books, Boulder, Colorado, and Spring Creek Press, Estes Park, Colorado. 2007.

Bailowitz, Richard and Douglas Danforth. *70 Common Butterflies of the Southwest.* Western National Parks Association, Tucson. 2002.

Burris, Judy and Wayne Richards. *The Life Cycles of Butterflies: From Egg to Maturity, a Visual Guide to 23 Common Garden Butterflies.* Storey Publishing, North Adams, Massachusetts. 2006

Gardening for Pollinators. Pamphlet published by the Arizona-Sonora Desert Museum with the Arizona Native Plant Society, Tucson. 1998.

Opler, Paul. *A Field Guide to Western Butterflies.* Houghton Mifflin, Boston. 1999.

Pyle, Robert Michael. *Handbook for Butterfly Watchers.* Houghton Mifflin, Boston. 1984.

Schappert, Phil. *A World for Butterflies: Their Lives, Behavior and Future.* Firefly Books, Buffalo, New York. 2000.

Shepherd, M.D., D.M. Vaughan, and S.H. Black, eds. *Red List of Pollinator Insects of North America.* CD-ROM Version 1 (May 2005). The Xerces Society for Invertebrate Conservation, Portland, Oregon.

Stewart, Bob, Priscilla Brodkin, and Hank Brodkin. *Butterflies of Arizona: A Photographic Guide.* West Coast Lady Press, Arcata, California. 2001.

Sutton, Patricia Taylor and Clay Sutton. *How to Spot Butterflies.* Houghton Mifflin, Boston. 1999.

Acknowledgments

Thanks to Stephen Buchmann, Chris Kline, Paul Opler, and Chip Taylor who gave generously of their time and technical knowledge. Thanks also to the National Park Service specialists who were enthusiastic and helpful resources.
Copyright © 2009 by Rose Houk
ISBN: 978-1-58369-122-9
Published by Western National Parks Association. The net proceeds from Western National Parks Association publications support educational and research programs in the national parks.

Receive a free Western National Parks Association catalogue, featuring hundreds of publications. Email: info@wnpa.org or visit www.wnpa.org.

Written by Rose Houk
Edited by Abby Mogollón
Designed by Dawn DeVries Sokol
Photography by: front cover: Rick and Nora Bowers; page 3: Rick and Nora Bowers; page 4: Tom and Pat Leeson; page 5: Sally King (top left), Rick and Nora Bowers (top right), Sally King (bottom); page 6: Rick and Nora Bowers; page 7: Tom and Pat Leeson (top), Rick and Nora Bowers (bottom); page 8: Sally King; page 9: Rick and Nora Bowers (top left and middle), Richard Day (top right and all bottom images); page 10: Richard Day (top), Sally King (bottom), page 11: Richard Day (top), Rick and Nora Bowers, (bottom); page 12: Rick and Nora Bowers (top), Kitchin and Hurst/leesonphoto (bottom); page 13: Rick and Nora Bowers (top left), Richard Day (top middle and right), Fred Siskind (center), Sally King (bottom left), Rick and Nora Bowers (bottom right); page 14: Kitchin and Hurst/leesonphoto; page 15: Allan Morgan; page 16: Rick and Nora Bowers; page 17: George H.H. Huey (top), Rick and Nora Bowers (middle); page 18: Sally King (top), Tom and Pat Leeson (bottom); page 19: Rick and Nora Bowers; page 20: Richard Day.
Illustrations by Paul Mirocha
Map by Paul Mirocha
Printing by Four Colour Imports, Ltd.
Printed in China

FREQUENTLY
ASKED QUESTIONS
ABOUT
Butterflies

How long do most butterflies live? Do butterflies migrate?
What kinds of plants do butterflies prefer? What do butterflies eat? Learn the
answers to these questions and many others in this easy-to-use book.
Concise text and colorful photos and illustrations help you learn about
these lovely, flying wisps of color.

WESTERN
NATIONAL PARKS
ASSOCIATION

www.wnpa.org

$ 5.95

ISBN 978-158369122-9
90000>

9 781583 691229

Printed in China